Free Verse Editions

Edited by Jon Thompson

Also by Carolyn Guinzio

Spoke & Dark

Quarry

West Pullman

SPINE

Poems

Carolyn Guinzio

Parlor Press
Anderson, South Carolina
www.parlorpress.com

Parlor Press LLC, Anderson, South Carolina, 29621

Printed in the United States of America
S A N: 2 5 4 - 8 8 7 9

Library of Congress Cataloging-in-Publication Data

Guinzio, Carolyn.
[Poems. Selections]
Spine : poems / Carolyn Guizno.
pages ; cm
ISBN 978-1-60235-754-9 (softcover : acid-free paper)
I. Title.
PS3607.U5426A6 2016
811'.6--dc23

2015029136

Cover design by Carolyn Guinzio
Cover Image: "Lamp" by Carolyn Guinzio
Back Cover Image: "Faux Fir" by Carolyn Guinzio
Printed on acid-free paper.

Parlor Press, LLC is an independent publisher of scholarly and trade titles in print and multimedia formats. This book is available in paperback and ebook formats from Parlor Press on the World Wide Web at http://www.parlorpress.com or through online and brick-and-mortar bookstores. For submission information or to find out about Parlor Press publications, write to Parlor Press, 3015 Brackenberry Drive, Anderson, South Carolina, 29621, or email editor@parlorpress.com.

Contents

SPINE

We make a dwelling in the evening air,
In which being there together is enough.

—*Wallace Stevens*

A Post On This Thread

I marked every kick in the book.
On the last day, we walked. Morels
new to the aboveground were still
malformed brains on their stems.
Mostly, the round mouths of deer
had appeared, breathed and then bitten,
beaten us there, leaving nothing
but a taunting stalk. The bittern
made a swallowing sound. Fear
and contentment meeting in its throat,
the quail made a queer feather-blanket
purr, but stayed outside the eye's reach.
We all know the old will settle their senses
on a plane beyond pain, but later.
Now, it was just beginning to change.
A towhee kept saying: The playground
is empty, but the swing still swings.
We were weaving over the field.
Wobbling vultures were waiting their turn,
and the shadows moved like swings.

Terra Inferma

The only thing moving
was the eye of the python
while it waited in the pines
and palmettos to break
down its gain. What
is the sound of twenty
bikes passing? Spokes
in the sphere of the snake's
eye spinning, the equi-
lateral sections of the pie
chart are forever
switching around:
the little and the large,
the fallen and those
that the world chose
not to swallow yet.
They only appear
in your rear view
mirror— wiry, quiet,
brightly striped. At night,
you won't hear them
until you are already gone.

Swedish Fish

I ran over a shadow,
and the car went *bump*.
In the back, the kid
was worrying his sweet
tooth with the tip
of his tongue.
What he wanted
was to catch me
in a generous mood.
He saw all the signs:
Vote Yes, Speed Table,
No Exit, and he mumbled
with disgruntled syncopation,
as in *sazzifrazzin laws*
and laws, the dark
graphics standing
between us and the wildness
we shed to get through.
What he wanted
was to stay
in the shadow of the fish
crow, hooking
left where they let
down the guard
rail, to crash
through the sage-
brush and angry
old trees that wait
to be thrown
into relief.
Oh, there are Great
rules I want
him to keep,
so I broke the little
red fish into halves
and sent them flying
into the back
when he opened his mouth
to speak.

Blu-ray, May-fly

There are shades
only the short-

lived can discern,
—unseen by the fat-

spanned who store
so little in their vast

cache of hours—
Ephemeral

gradations on the disc
too vivid for the life-

is-long panorama—
that other wavelength

from which time's
luxurious sweep is seen,

a lower-dwelling
definition of what is central

as more than mere
being, but *To Be*,

too high for the eyes
of those with wings

and limbs that don't tear
from encountering the air

and for whom the day's sky
is not every possible sky.

Password

A key broke its neck
in the lock. Around
back, a nest of blue

bombing jays would peck
at our ducking
heads and flash

away with our hair
in their beaks. Yellow-
jackets blocked the way

to the basement
with a quiver of stings.
There was something

sharp and furry curled
around a rung
of the ladder. The mud-

spattered skylight
was cracked
by webs, and half-

sleeping bats
lined the chimney
with the angles

of their ears. If only
the windows knew us
from a storm

or a thief who would bash
in the glass and spirit
away what is ours—

away over the petrified
prints that waited
deep down under the grass.

Stone Chairs In The Waterfall

The devices were buried
in rice, and the grains

would fatten
by wicking the river

that had wound its way
into the ear-

phone jack and lens.
The water was laced

with metal and lead.
The sun steamed

the names and numbers
into the mist made

by the falls. The falls
look blue from the boat,

but white in the satellite
image. The noise

of the falls was white,
and they waited in stone

chairs beneath them.
The sun made a prism

of the mist. The blue
tint faded from the faces

and the faces began
to go blank.

What What The The Satellite Google Car Sees Saw

Warren is burying a key
beneath the skeleton trees.
An earring in a tree
A soft shoulder
All the world's a grave.
He says, the mystery
A horse on its side
A dip
at the center of things
is the fragmented spark
A helicopter landing on a hospital roof
A falling rock
of the dead. We want
to be remembered.
A girl on a trestle
A crosswind deviling dust
Warren is peeling the husk
and silk from the ears
A penny rolling into a grate
A bump
of silver corn. He will give them
all away. He is rolling the snow
A mug on the roof of a van
An egret on one leg
to make stripes of green
that say, from the sky, I am I—

I Heard A Phone Buzz

I heard a Phone buzz— when I died—
The Signal and Glow hurtled down
From the Sky—Between Blinks
Of the Tower— A Great red Eye—

Encased in metal Thorns— It seemed
A Wounded tree. Turning face-
Down on the table— The Phone did not know
I did not need to know— the Day's high—

The Night's low— A moan from Deep in the works—
A Window's frozen blue cracked Screen—
Suspended in a corner was the Symbol
Of a Burning Moon or Please Do Not Disturb—

Here's How It's Going To Work

Something is going
to arc through the sky.
It will land behind
the tree line ridge,

near the tall dead one—
Not the one you know,
with the oaks and crows,
and not the one I know,

with the sparrow's
brown and gray blinks
in the maples—but the one
things fall behind now.

From where we stand
— you in the field,
unfolding from over
an orbit of rocks,

me in the open door-
way, tilting to better
encompass the dome—
We will move toward

the phantom thump
and streak that bats
maneuver to circum-
vent, across the timeline,

past sunken remnants
of rooms— and arrive
together. And together
we will tamp the ground

down at a place that will
bear no scar. The marker
we leave will be scratched
with both our names.

A Philosophy

The continuum is a rope
And ocurrences are beads
And you will see yourself moving
Toward one that is dark and will be
Difficult to move through
And every aspect of the rope
Will be intensified: The blue
Thread's small weave, its color
Against the asphalt (the bead
Is the color of asphalt)
And certain other
Occurrences in the past will come
To look the same way (being
Followed from the train)
As if the rope has been
Struck like a cicada or guitar
You will have to keep moving
Toward the darkness (because
Oblivion is the only Other)
And into the darkness
And through it and the continuum
Will seem to slow down
And the darkness will still
Cling to you and leave
Its traces

On the rope

As you drag

Yourself away
From it
And it
Will never
Be gone
Because it was

Always
There.

It
will
never
be
gone
because
it
was
always
there

The Pines

The Pines

One two.

There is a ligature,

The ant eats the nectar from the aphid

and there is *begin again.*

The man eats the nectar from the ant

We were in the car
with a fly.

To walk is to seek

When the fly first finds itself inside,
it is wild.

a pure form of being

And the signs have tails.
Move read as *maze*. And *Eyes* and *yes*.

To know what was thrown in the river
knows that the river is only the bed

And the movement of the car
in its nimbleness left a heavenly nimbus

To know the name of the flower

on everything. There are fields.
And the houses were there before the road.

To know the name of the bug

And we said how beautiful the houses would be
if they were where they couldn't be seen.

A device.

First

We were both there when it happened. Or, I was there when you told me about it,

something

or you were listening to me tell you about it, and once one of us said it out loud to the other, it became an idea. The soon-to-be beings that we called into being

had to happen

sat up from where they were resting on the backs of the ghosts standing on one leg in the marshes. In those days, we went to the marshes to see beautiful things

to move us away

we had never seen before. We would stop unpacking the boxes (which meant we were staying [together]) and walk out to the marshes where curlews and cormorants watched us arrived with something that seemed like fear. The moment

from ourselves.

the evening breeze reached us from the hills where it came to exist, we went back to our room and opened the huge window together to let them in.

Experience as sight.

If what happened to someone one day in the woods is an idea that matters to

We backed

everyone, out of fairness to the almost unearthly beauty of the pines, the sharp ravines and clear waterfalls, the sharp and clear features of the sketch stapled to

away from

the trees at the edge of the woods, the spots on thrushes and oven birds blurring in the stillness around them in the scrub when they are waiting to be sure it's safe to

an idea

emerge from where they are hiding in what seems like fear— the ghosts pushed

and ended up

their way into the space.

in the pines.

An unexpected event.

And then it begins

Slip

to slow.

your

And then it begins

arm

to snow

A slowing, a lowering. The fly flies less and lands again lower.

into

A shirt was hanging on a hook on the door.

the

Remember slipping your arm into the sleeve?

sleeve.

Refrigerator door.

Something is moving in the wall.

You're

Something

It only matters if you are alone, and if it is otherwise silent.

going

is

The sound of a house settling its weight onto the plot

to

is *nothing*. Something moving in the wall is *probably nothing.*

moving

Spaces are all smaller than you will remember them.

be

How many things did you recognize for what they were
at the time? The thing that matters more is always

through

coming from another direction. Because things look different

sorry

from this angle. Sound was coming through

the wall

the wall. Yes, spending the night alone meant the senses

someday

were tuned to the soon-to-be.
You're going to be sorry someday.

A pure form of being.

Some things will (not) be reborn. Some things
How
remain unnamed (a flower is a flower, a bug is a bug)
beautiful
an unexpected event). Here is the realm in which you enter
the things
an idea through the eye. How beautiful the things
we've
we don't own by proximity.
never
Here, slip your arm into the sleeve.
seen

An unexpected event.

We backed away

into the pines

into the ghosts

into the soon-to-be

A Descant

The onset of sun-
set was the low
note of a bitter
day. Our voices rose
and rose until hounds
began a symphony
of sympathy agony.
The red February
skies were red
through the eye,
not only the heart-
shaped wrapper
we tore from around
the heart-shaped
box bought after
mid-month for half-
off. *It takes so very*
long for things
to leave the blood—
So said my dead
aunt from where
she sat way-back-
when with cake
and black coffee.
Now, we looked
to the kettle of black
vultures breathing
in the cold upper
reaches of sky.
But they didn't
whistle. They sighed.

From The Trees

Cicadas are ideas
clicking in the trees.

In her hat, a hiker
is picking her way

through a trail, keeping
the brushed-aside brush

from slapping. Sometimes
things fall from the trees.

A sense, through her hat,
that something has landed

is troubling in its subtlety.
What does a husk weigh?

She is suddenly heavier,
in the way she was lighter

when her pocket was picked
on the train. Stealing away

from the trees, she is not
attached to a name,

but something is hitched
to her hat. Where was *she*

when *she* was gripping
the infinite margin of a brim

with hooked feet?
By the time she returns

to the car, she will have
returned to herself. She will

take off her hat and bat it
against her human leg.

Eat, Eat

She placed the baby
on the kitchen
scale. She called

the others for supper
and turned
to them, bleeding

from a slip of the knife
on the round end of a sweet
potato, orange as a red-

shouldered hawk.
It was nearly time
to bury the root

vegetables in the root
cellar for winter.
All winter, she listened

and watched for the end—
the crocuses and croaks,
the bloodroot. Cold

clumps of dirt clinging
to creases, potatoes
would lie side by side

with their curved middles
jutting up in the dark.
All winter, the baby,

raveling the swaddling,
would hold his cold
feet in his hands.

How To Take A Picture Of A Leaf /
/ Reciprocal Likes

I pick a riddled bois d'arc
        I like your baby
from the moldering
        You like my dad
floor of the woods
        I like your garden
and hold it by the stem
        You like my cat
against the sky— or, rather,
        I like your mirror
ask Charlotte to hold—
        You like my leaf
Her deeply beautiful
        I like your supper
hand alluding to the unseen
        You like my sky
being who is both in all
        I like your roses
senses of both: The long
        You like my fog
unlined lines of her fingers
        I like your birthday
attached to the sun-gleaming
        You like my beach
cane, blue light blazing through
        I like your link
the holes gold worms bore.
        You like my barn
The leaf, in its half-ghosted state,
        I like your shadow
may be lovelier than it was whole,
        You like my bird
I know, but still, I can't stand
        I like your book
the sight of my late-summer hand.

Dead Links

A hammer was wrapped
in a canvas bag,

muddying the middle
C. I think you're trying

to tell me something. Once,
I stood near the river

so long, I heard two of them
whispering in a tree. He said,

It's about so much more
than the sound. I think

he was trying to be funny.
A group of them were shuffling

onto the top deck of a purple bus.
I think they were in for a treat.

Sharp-ended ice was raining
from the awnings of interest,

and every arthritic had faith
it was true: they knew without

having to see. All the angora
berets were just so, the lavender

and the gray, on the way
to the big store downtown.

Gone comes the grievous
moan from the grate.

I think I can hear it now.
Gone. When the angles

evaporate, all that remains
is a never-ending round of

Think Of How History Will Remember You

When the fever
inhabits all
of the cabin's
inhabitants.

When you are cowering
in the woods
beyond the reach
of our shouts.

When we are telling you
about lifting
your dog into the car,
on three.

When the hands
that clutch at you
are not
clutching.

When you are
too paper-lean
to lean upon
the podium.

When the room
is emptied of every-
thing, and you
wake up on the floor.

When your stack
of papers
opens up
to speak.

When a stranger
falls asleep
on your shoulder
on the train.

We Followed The Gaze Of A Stranger And Saw

Scaffolding dangling
from the twelfth story

for the eleventh time
this year. Lake winds

scraped at our faces,
and the metal scaffold

scraped at the brick.
A woman stood with her

purse and her personal
trainer, looking up.

He told her to hold
her eyes *right there*

for a count of ten,
and then let them rest

on the cracking cement
at her feet. It was

Thursday, a throwback
to all the other hard

winters we'd known.
Each one left a trace

on the face. *Where should*
I look when I wake? she asked.

Start with darkness, end
with light, he smiled his un-

lined smile and offered a white
balloon on a white ribbon.

It slipped from her freezing
hand and popped on the bottom

of the elevated track. Be
the first person to like this.

Spire

Why does the highway go quiet sometimes?
We're starting all over from nothing.
Why do pillbugs gather to die?
How good the rug-world felt beneath them.
Why is the sidewalk buckling there?
We were warned by the orange wooden horses.
Why can't I sleep tonight?
The senses help each other fill the space.
Why do the rivers and our palms look alike?
There used to be a footbridge made of pine.
Why do we go through the door into darkness?
The spots on the wings look like eyes.
Why is the nest filled with ribbons and webs?
Only from the top step of the ladder.
Why did the tooth break off in the apple?
It was nothing but a list of names.
Why does the curtain close over the screen?
The curtain closed over the screen.

Drift

i. / age

Have you ever heard migrating cranes going over in the dark, using their voices? Have you ever put a red dot on a dollar bill and gotten it back in another state? Don't you know there's a war on? Where do you keep your loose change? We had to wait to hear from each other. Don't spend the pennies that someone you loved once touched.

ii. spin /

Have you got a pen?
From your place, you're going to want to make a right.
Make a left at the first blue sign.
There's a cemetery with an iron arch with a lamb in a circle in the center.
The road curves there. The road forks after that. Take the westernmost tine toward the house with a pig statue in the front yard.
When you see the "End State Maintenance" notice, swing to the right toward the red-fenced field filled with smoking pipes.
You want to pass the mailbox in the shape of a chicken.
Be on the lookout for a stone house with a blue outbuilding by a gravel road that dips down almost out of sight.
Watch for the shorthorns that like to stand in the middle of the one-lane bridge.
You have to pick left or right after that.
Go toward the guy in a mallard hat fishing off the end of the ramp.
If you see a pair of swallows with mud in their mouths, you missed the turn.

iv. snow /

Once, there was a woman who wanted to document everything about her small house, the small field behind it. There were three snowfalls that year. In one, the snow piled up on the branches. In another, it gleamed in the next-day sun. She walked into the field, her boots stable for a second with each step, before they fell into six inch holes of their own making. A thin layer of ice on top of the snow. What did it remind her of— A wedding cookie, a Mozartkugel, a Jordan almond? She needed to remember this snow. She bent down and slid a rock across it. Something winged hopped into her periphery and she turned to it with such force that her eyes sailed away from her and quivered for a moment on the snow before sinking into darkness.

Wiki June // Balcony at Evening

The heat cycle
sighs through the pipes.
Roadside clingstone
and freestone are gone.
When the season is over,
the cloverleaf exit, the stand,
abandoned, may cease to exist,
but we are not there to know.

There must be upward moving air
for freezing rain to fall.
All powers fail
from the weight. The patoo
and pontoon may be eerily synced,
whistling in the sound, wrapped
in the banana's waterproof leaves,
but we are not there to know.

Flood frost, wind frost,
radiation frost. The crystal
spines scatter their bone-
drawn glow. A symmetry in sea
urchin feet may be seen
in the dead on the red-
flagged sand,
but we are not there to know.

A man was chasing
a woman down
the alley.
In the setting
sun, steam
from the neighbor's
pot of noodles
came to seem,

for a second,
from the second
story, like something
you could hold
in your fist
against your ear.
The headlight beams
of trains as they turn

would be filled with
the shapes voices have,
if voices have shape,
filled with our breath
and the breath
of beings who run
through alleys, stories
together in the steam.

Undo

The expert returned my call
and said there was little
time left to repent. The timer
went off, so I turned off
the timer, but its phantom
kept on— It burned
in the ear. The flash

that had burned in the eye
kept on, but the lens had left
the room. For the ear
or the egg: a candling.
Someone was tapping
at the door. The window
was closed: in came a ghost

of a draft. My ears
were burning. The bottom
of the pan sounded hollow,
and I heard the tunneling
heat. The boy at the door
selling history books
said, *How much do you*

care? The expert knew
about love, pain, and anger;
the boy with the books
about love, guilt, and cash.
I tapped an egg on the edge
of the sink and put my ear
to the pan: It was burning.

The boy was cold:
He had broken the spine,
and he offered to take
off half. The expert
was sorry: Time
had run out. The current
version was saved.

The Pleasure of the Text // Book of Cells

Driver with pitching
bed hitched on truck,
of thee I text, rubble flung
into mirrror and wind-
shields of your followers.
You have broken, driver,
the glass between us.
It is broken and I will
be late. I frame
in my app the open
eye of the half-
dead fish on your plate.
Send, send, signs
of sighs. Blue lines
gutter from my eyes.

Congratulations! Condolences.
Condolences. Congratulations!
Congratulations! Condolences.
Condolences. Congratulations!
Congratulations! Condolences.
Condolences. Congratulations!
Congratulations! Condolences.
Condolences. Congratulations!
Congratulations! Condolences.
Condolences. Congratulations!
Congratulations! Condolences.
Condolences. Congratulations!
Congratulations! Condolences.
Condolences. Congratulations!
Congratulations! Condolences.

Optics

I am exactly where I was when you left. I am thinking
about opening the windows. I am thinking about opening
a gift shop on the beach. We never step into the same
building twice. In the winter, people in cold cities cut
through lobbies of buildings, and the white floors turn
into slush. When we are cold in the winter, we don't believe
we will ever be warm again. I am thinking it doesn't look good.
I am listening to the highway, and I am listening to the sirens.
They are testing the system, and the dogs are barking.
A range of emotion can be heard in the barks. Studies
concluding animals have feelings are presented as if they are
surprising. I am looking at a cat through the door. The cat
is tracking a dragonfly through the sky. I am worried about
the children, and I am worried that we won't have time to talk
about how we are worried about our parents. I am imagining
the recluse under the bed and the widow between the window
panes. I am trying to remember where the fire ladder is.
I am starting to think we didn't plan well enough. I am
worried about what you will think when you get home
and discover that I am exactly where I was when you left.

White Noise // Options for Rural WiFi

We turned
on the fans
for sleeping.
Calls of tree
frogs got caught
in the blades.
Three crow's feet
gripped the wires.
Theirs are not
the only voices
cutting through
the air. The smoke
alarm would sound
like a bread
truck backing
up at dawn
many flat miles
away. We can't

Some residents
of the white
spots on the maps
have found it useful
to send the tendril
ends of the atmopshere
down into the steam
that streams
from your lonely chimney.
At night, the stars
form a broad
band of blue
in the black patches
not caught in the casting
marked by the surrounding
towers. Be patient.
They say things
are improving

predict which

all the time.

direction the draft

Was this page

will send out

helpful?

signals of the actual.

Yes ☐ *No* ☐

Process

If I wanted to mention the flowers, I would say the marigolds seem to be kneeling at the feet of the plants that matter more. They seem to be leaning against one another. Exiles and immigrants make little worlds to replicate big old worlds. They lean. In supposing a supporting post could be removed, the rehabber was positing beauty as supreme. Or just the present. There is supposedly a moment when thinking outpaces the body, an instant of suspension, an outsider trying to blend in with the crowd of possibilities. But wait and when everything falls back into place, everything has not fallen. The surveyors are marking with math the exact degrees by which a place becomes another. They make a vertical mark under which the horizontal continues. That partial instant of dissonant friction is where our land begins. Be sure to bring these directions when you are coming over for drinks. The kids made a message for the satellite shot, and you don't want to know what it said. It can only be seen from a great distance at a single instant a blue lens lasers its way from a humbling height to the earth. None of us wants to go there.

A Portrait

Sketch me, she said
breathlessly. It was
too dark for dark
shadows, her rope
arms bending
to straighten her hair.

The water stopped
rushing to examine
a rock. Or the rock
insisted its existence
be acknowledged,
and the water bent

to mirror its features.
He tilted her chin
to obscure
the asymmetrical,
unbeautiful nature
of her eyes.

The cherub legs
on the concrete moon
garden bench were aglow,
though the sweet
alyssum sought asylum
in its own folds,

shrinking away
from the touch,
not of the moon,
but of the Sylvania
Roadster high pressure
sodium vapor street lamp

that sensed it was time.
She grabbed at the book
to see, and a lead comet
streaked her face
where he hadn't finished
shading in her bones.

A Hairpin Turn

We felt a drop
(of ice)
in the tone
(in the wind)
of the talk
(it cut)
it was becoming
(the leaves)
something
(into shreds)
that couldn't
(and nothing)
be stopped
(could stop it).

We looked
(up)
at each other
(and it fell)
across the walk
(into our eyes)
and we fell
(the ice)
into the dark
(was becoming)
where the salt
(permanent)
couldn't melt
(and delicate)
the ice.

Spiders // The Plsr of the Txt

You or someone
who looked like you

Roads fan out from the house
to places we lived as children
to places we visited alone before we met

just passed me on Mount
Comfort Road in a car

to places we went together
to places we long to return to
to places we hope never to see again

with a special black
bear plate and a human

to places we would rather be living
to places you love that I've never seen
to places I love that you've never seen

rights sticker in the center
of the bumper.

Voices stream into the house
of people who once were important to you
of people who once were important to me

When you tear
a sentence apart

of loved ones living borders away
of loved ones buried borders away
of animals buried by a cedar in the yard

and put it back together,
it looks at you eerily

of ancestors, telling us what we do wrong
of descendants, telling us what we did wrong
Shadows stream into the house

wrong. I met the reflection
of your eyes in the mirror

Light pours out from the house
when the sun drags slowly over
when we stand still in the window

for a second. For the record,

I turned off and parked

when the sun is streaming rain off the roof
when we are pretending to sleep
when the sun is crossed by the moon

to send this. I wonder
if you knew it was me.

when we wait a long time at the door
when the sun is cold and pale
when we seen to be frozen in place

A Problem of Philosophy

The idea was to set
aside the idea
of the shell
and the hermit's crawl.
Stepping around
treacherous seaside
rocks, we returned
to the problem of universals.
Somewhere above us,
the cowbird hatchling
was pushing the flycatcher
out of the nest.
The cowbird was catching
its breath. Thus the law
of contradiction is not
merely about thoughts.
The baby feels the moon
has a mystical place
in its arrival: It blinks
at slivers of dawn
on the silver water
from which it crawled.
It blinks at the belief
that every event
has a cause.
The flycatcher opens
its mouth.

Because the ocean

is a symbol scattered over the page,
we stopped when we were driving
and decided to stay. In the trunk
there was a trunk full of books,
and we lived on so little: Hand-
to-mouth, close-to-the-bone,
except for the bank. We hit
the beach first and return
at shorter intervals since
the sea means the end.
In the end, we turned
around. We were not
ready to become part
of it, the great, dark
wave on the edge. We
were getting tired of it.
We didn't want to admit
that we missed being in a
central place. We began to
think that everyone had quit
talking about us and how we
had made this radical decision
to live the way someone else we
encountered was living instead of
the way they were living. We had to
point ourselves out to them again. We
faced the center of things and hit return.

It's Too Quiet In Here

A sparrow mistook
a light for the light
of day. A contractor
penciled *Transitional*
Space on the plans.
A woman parked
next to the airport
and stood on top
of her truck.
In an empty office,
a fax inched out
of the printer.
The wind knocked
over a metal bucket.
Spirals at the end
of a vending
machine turned
to let down the chips.
Everyone in the sub-
way pitched right.
A blue crayon melted
on the welcome mat.
The timer for the timed
test went off. A pilot
light went out. Every-
one on the bus pitched
left. A shade slapped
open, untouched, and dust
flew up into the sun.

Underpainting

(We keep returning to the surface.)

The neck of the girl in *Girl Reading* is angled

over a book. Light does not rise from the page

and through the eye enter an interior gray.

The red sun is balanced on the other hand.

In short, the sky. In theory, the creek at the edge

of the grounds, the gray waves conveyed

by fronds of rain on paned and warping glass.

Behind this world, that other—

Where a spine divides the hemispheres.

(We return to the surface,

unable to say what we've seen.)

The Root

An estuary was curled up on the map,
and the edges of the map curled up.
That day, we borrowed from foreboding
and threw another omen out the window.
It landed on a shoulder full of half-
eroded links. How do you arrive at a place
of placing your foot upon the ground unshod
where the earth itself is bound in tar?
The exits are tendrils, curling away
from the road like the ribbons ripped along
the scissor's blade, and here is where
we find them: Open-eyed, arms holding
their knees up near the heart, holding
in their soles all the miles of the world
a pair of soles can hold. Stop speaking
in riddles, and put back on your boots.

A Night Letter Is Cheaper Than A Day Letter

A night letter is cheaper than a day letter because what it contains (it says by being a night letter) can wait until morning. It is sent in the night, but it won't arrive until morning, the implication being that the worst has happened and nothing can be done (*this*, note, was the fifty word mark, not counting this note or the title) to change this fact. Someone stood somewhere in the dark, perhaps with some kind of light cast on them, composing the content of the night letter, a letter of less than fifty words. If there was a phone booth, they stood in the phone booth, dictating into the phone (*this*, note, was the hundred word mark, not counting this note or the title) the fifty words. It has to be fifty words or less. In fifty words, any news about which nothing can be done before morning can be reported, speaking into the speaker of a phone in a phone booth in the dark, under the overhead light. If we think for a moment (*this*, note, was the one-fifty mark, not counting this note or the title) about news about which nothing can be done until morning, we realize we would rather not think about it. A night letter is cheaper than a day letter because if you have to send news in the night about something about which nothing can be done until morning, you should (*this*, note, was the two-hundred mark, not counting this note or the title) be able to do so at a discounted rate. Someone is sleeping not knowing the night letter will be there in the morning, not thinking yet about what has happened about which nothing can be done until morning. Tomorrow night someone will not be able to stop— Full stop. (*this*, note, was the two-fifty mark, not counting this note or the title).

Selected Emptiness*

A cat grabbed a fledgling by the feet.
A storm shook a fledgling from a tree.
The sky caught a fledgling as it fell.
A snake bit a fledgling in the neck.
A hawk seized a fledgling by the head.
A bird caught a fledgling as it fell.
A wasp stung a fledgling in the wing.
A crow plucked a fledgling from the grass.
The grass caught a fledgling as it fell.
A truck hit a fledgling in the road.
A stone hit a fledgling in the eye.
A branch caught a fledgling as it fell.
A cowbird pushed a fledgling from the nest.
The eye burned a fledgling with the lens.
The wind caught a fledgling as it fell.

*If your story ends with sorrow rather than hope,
reverse the wind and the sky.

Live Stream / / Sent from my iPhone

Here is the run-
          Sending this to mail
off from the flood.
          because you can't hear
Here is the flipped-
          text sound over screaming
over high-profile
          in hallway at work
vehicle. Someone
          sending it everywhere
set a white fine
          since Android is dead
bone-china cup,
          and everything goes
trembling on its plate,
          to the Galaxy
in the center
          am getting there
of the square
          hope
as a symbol
          you are too
of endurance
          can't rest until
or a joke. Between
          conveyances are
the dense, low-
          docked for night
hanging clouds
          forgive
there was whispering,
          brevity
though the mayor
          corrections
kept thundering,
          mistakes

cease and desist.
                Sent
We need a chance
                from
to catch up. Between
                my
earth and sky, for a time,
                iPhone
a buffer, a buffer…

Match Game

There isn't enough
blank in the world
to get us through
the blankness.
On the ramble,
you caught yourself
on the prickly
pear when you fell.
You caught yourself
about to say blank.
I kissed your palm.
Dora said it was a sign
from blank. Dora
was so dumb,
she misread the map
and led the hiking tour
straight into blank.
It was getting dark,
and the cars were so distant
from the weary blanks
of our faces, our rambled-
out feet. The circling meat-
eaters of day were being
quietly replaced
by the blanks
of night. Dora
was so dumb,
she said this test
would reveal the true
blank of our blanks.
Dora is confusing
the blank with the bones,
we whispered
to each other
as we crawled
under the blank
to stay warm.

We Hated Novels

We loved novels, but we hated novels with an *I* that was transparently the writer.

We hated novels with an *I* that seemed to be the writer and was superior to all the other characters.

We hated novels with an *I* that seemed to be the writer working out their personal issues through the plot.

We hated novels with an *I* that seemed to be taking revenge on people who had slighted the writer in life by sentencing their characters to terrible fates.

We hated novels with all brilliant male characters and all vacuous female characters.

We hated novels that allowed us to imagine the writer in their room thinking up ways to subject the characters to terrible fates.

We hated novels that held their characters in contempt.

We hated novels that used human misery, not in service of something great, but rather to exploit the baser voyeuristic tendencies of potential book buyers.

We hated novels that were spun like cotton candy around a paper core of research.

We hated novels with no subtlety.

We hated novels with no empathy.

We hated novels with predictable endings.

We hated novels with endings that allowed us to imagine the writer trying to surprise us.

We hated novels that didn't know how to end.

We hated when a novel we loved ended, because we loved novels. We loved them so much.

re: No Subject

Within five seconds,
you will be redirected

to the site of the earliest
sparks. Guards are sleeping

in the haystacks to keep
elk from the cattle's fodder.

We meant to put you
in the brackets, [first name].

Please add your name
to the list. Generations

of Americans have looked
up from washing dishes

through the window
over the sink and met

the eye of a single coyote
before it turned back into

the woods, or turned back
into whatever it actually was.

Covered burrows riddle
the fields, and something

breathes in the burrows.
If you are not redirected

within five seconds,
try climbing the tower

and dragging your eyes
slowly over the grass.

System Preferences // Sleep Corners

A fever
A window
A lake

Reading
in
bed

The dock — like the dock
we argued on in the dark
at the end of that day —
should rest on the marina
of an intercoastal waterway,
fish visible between the slats,
surfacing to eat saltines
shook down out of bags
by the kids we brought
to see the place they escaped,
half-panicked gulls giving
the fish a ten-second lead
before the screaming, the wind
knocking anchoring ropes
against metal poles, yellow
floats below our feet, the kids
catching themselves by their palms,
their eyes to the slats, while we,
in our minds, are seeing them
from underneath.

The first one
awake, stays
still, listening

a palm
on her back
in unmoved light

Carrion, Hooded, or Fish

One who watches while another steals

It's been twelve minutes since I saw you, and seven since the cawing stopped as you rounded the corner. The *you* to whom I refer never looked up from reading a text made from a tree, or down from a tree filled with twigs curled and crossed into letters.

A metronome started clicking its caws the second you turned your glass eye to me. We were sitting at desks made of trees, or in trees with parts that had been used up. There was a kitten sleeping under your desk, you reached under to fish it out.

You said it makes it easier to keep track. The kitten tracked things through the sky: Mayflies that crumpled under its gaze, satellites. You said, *eventually*— meaning we are hurtling. I could have used my time if not for the *you-are-almost-out-of-time-you-are*

When I looked at your glass eye, I saw reflected in its convexity a stick made into a U. This is how they make a bed out of them. We gave off heat. We went swimming in a painting of a pool on a wooden floor. We stopped when it started to storm.

You turned to me with a glass bead in your beak, making the clicking sound that was one of a hundred sounds I'd known you to make. After every hundred clicks, something turns over. I try to forget, but I find myself counting and waiting.

On a branch in the western sky, you were resting in front of the moon. I could look at you, or I could look at the moon. I looked at the moon. I was in a second story window. Someone was looking up at me. He said, *if you can see me, I can see you.*

This is not necessarily true. An aperture the size of a glass eye in the wood would allow me to see without being seen, my pupil a nothingness you look down into. The moon rose across the minutes, small and bright, cracked by the black branches.

Mode

There is no *there*
or where I can reach you.

Are you sleeping
on the wing over grid

and field, carted
by the lullaby of a cloud-

to-cloud-contrail
I can see from the ground

but don't want to dwell on
for long? The crated dogs

blink, forlorn. No joke:
it's easier for them to reach

the end of memory.
When the cabin opens

and you find your footing
on some other cracked plate

than this, it will seem
as if nothing has changed.

Pick a Card

Of what corruption
did the Queen
whisper in your ear?

That she never
ages, concealed
in the deepest

branch?
That between
the stacks, flat

sheets of whistling
air move like spine-
flattened cats

under a door? These
were your instructions:
Write your number

on this crumpled
paper and kick it
forward toward

the horizon. Try
to remember
your number.

Twist your neck
in the direction
of every peripheral

flash. What did
the Queen just tuck
into her bellows?

Look at all my small
mistakes, she blinks.
What rises before you

while you're turned
to the side? Your number.
Your number is up.

I Wish I Could Have Seen It Once Last Time

Summer began to become fall and became summer again and then fall, but we could feel the shifting, a gradual moving forward. Then we came here, and nothing changes. They say it changes, the people who have always lived here, but they are more sensitive to the subtleties of this geography. I don't think I'll have enough time to become so sensitive to the subtleties of this geography that I could tell the difference between a late winter and an early spring. It's never going to snow, and I wish I could have seen it one last time. You are supposed to move into the margin before you move out of the margin. You are supposed to look before you at what I imagine is a sea, but what is behind you I imagine is also a sea. You aren't supposed to look back, but I want to.

Cover Art

—A Dedication

Charlotte fell asleep in a chair.
Warren shielded his eyes from the sun.
Davis carried a saw through the yard.
Charlotte cleaned the bristles of her brush.
Warren hesitated on the stairs.
Davis broke down the cages.
Charlotte disappeared around a corner.
Warren untangled a cord.
Davis talked on the phone in the greenhouse.
Charlotte picked up the cat.
Warren closed the door to his room.
Davis fell asleep in a chair.

The Moving Walkway Is Ending

We are not here. My fellow-
assemblages of cells and I thread
our minds through the loops
of our bodies, and thus the terminal
burden is eased. All that is here
is what remains here: The house-
fly composed near the edge
of an ear, dragging its legs
down its face. House finches wait
in the buzzing eaves for night.
Their gaze is fixed on the sky,
and a flickering phosphorous grazes
the eye. Cold may threaten to reach
around the curve, but darkness
will never arrive. House ants, forever
dismantling a sweet, pull their glaze-
slowed claws through the grate.
They are here, but we are not.
We look down to step into the self.

Acknowledgments

Thank you to the editors of publications in which the following poems appeared:

Agni: "The Moving Walkway Is Ending"
Blackbird: "The Pines"
Bomb: "Dead Links," "I Heard A Phone Buzz When I Died," "Password"
Boston Review: "A Descant"
Carbon Culture Review: "White Noise/Options For Rural WiFi," "What What The The Satellite Google Car Sees Saw"
The Cortland Review: "Underpainting"
Diagram: "The Plsr of the Txt"
Diode: "A Portrait," "Pick A Card"
Entropy: "Selected Emptiness*," "Spire," Wiki-June/Balcony At Evening"
Harvard Review: "re: No Subject"
La Vague Journal: "Bottleneck/Redux," "System Preferences/Sleep Corners," "The Pleasure of the Text/Book of Cells"
New American Writing: "Here's How It's Going To Work," "It's Too Quiet In Here"
The New Yorker: "Swedish Fish"
Posit: "A Hairpin Turn," "Terra Inferma"
Storm Cellar: "Drift (ii)"
Thrush: "A Post On This Thread"
Verse: "Process"

"It's Too Quiet In Here" appeared on *Poetry Daily*

My gratitude to Chris Tokar, Jennifer Martenson, Sarah Vap, Elaine Equi, Bin Ramke, Jon Thompson, and David Blakesley.

Thank you Warren McCombs for the cover design ideas and author photo experiments.

For Davis, Warren and Charlotte— all my love.

About the Author

Carolyn Guinzio's previous collections are *West Pullman* (Bordighera, 2005), winner of the Bordighera Poetry Prize, *Quarry* (Parlor, 2008), and *Spoke & Dark* (Red Hen, 2012), winner of the To The Lighthouse/A Room Of Her Own Prize. Her writing and/or photography have appeared in many journals, including *Agni, Blackbird, Bomb, Boston Review, Harvard Review, New American Writing* and *The New Yorker*. A Chicago native, she lives in Fayetteville, Arkansas with her husband, the poet Davis McCombs, and their two children. She is the text editor of *YEW: A Journal of Innovative Writing & Images By Women*. Find her online at carolynguinzio.tumblr.com

Photograph of the author by Warren McCombs.
Used by permission.

Free Verse Editions

Edited by Jon Thompson

13 ways of happily by Emily Carr
Between the Twilight and the Sky by Jennie Neighbors
Blood Orbits by Ger Killeen
The Bodies by Chris Sindt
The Book of Isaac by Aidan Semmens
Canticle of the Night Path by Jennifer Atkinson
Child in the Road by Cindy Savett
Condominium of the Flesh by Valerio Magrelli, trans. by Clarissa Botsford
Contrapuntal by Christopher Kondrich
Country Album by James Capozzi
The Curiosities by Brittany Perham
Current by Lisa Fishman
Dismantling the Angel by Eric Pankey
Divination Machine by F. Daniel Rzicznek
Erros by Morgan Lucas Schuldt
The Forever Notes by Ethel Rackin
The Flying House by Dawn-Michelle Baude
Instances: Selected Poems by Jeongrye Choi, translated by Brenda Hillman, Wayne de Fremery, & Jeongrye Choi
The Magnetic Brackets by Jesús Losada, translated by Michael Smith & Luis Ingelmo
A Map of Faring by Peter Riley
No Shape Bends the River So Long by Monica Berlin & Beth Marzoni
Pilgrimly by Siobhán Scarry
Physis by Nicolas Pesque, translated by Cole Swensen
Poems from above the Hill & Selected Work by Ashur Etwebi, translated by Brenda Hillman & Diallah Haidar
The Prison Poems by Miguel Hernández, translated by Michael Smith
Puppet Wardrobe by Daniel Tiffany
Quarry by Carolyn Guinzio
remanence by Boyer Rickel
Signs Following by Ger Killeen
Split the Crow by Sarah Sousa
Spine by Carolyn Guinzio
Spool by Matthew Cooperman
Summoned by Guillevic, translated by Monique Chefdor

Sunshine Wound by L. S. Klatt
These Beautiful Limits by Thomas Lisk
The Thinking Eye by Jennifer Atkinson
An Unchanging Blue: Selected Poems 1962–1975 by Rolf Dieter Brinkmann, translated by Mark Terrill
Under the Quick by Molly Bendall
Verge by Morgan Lucas Schuldt
The Wash by Adam Clay
We'll See by George Godeau, translated by Kathleen McGookey
What Stillness Illuminated by Yermiyahu Ahron Taub
Winter Journey [Viaggio d'inverno] by Attilio Bertolucci, translated by Nicholas Benson
Wonder Rooms by Allison Funk

www.ingramcontent.com/pod-product-compliance
Ingram Content Group UK Ltd.
Pitfield, Milton Keynes, MK11 3LW, UK
UKHW041644190726
13854UKWH00006B/2679

9 781602 357549